Neglected Defense

Mobilizing the Private Sector to Support Homeland Security

Stephen E. Flynn
Daniel B. Prieto

CSR NO. 13, MARCH 2006
COUNCIL ON FOREIGN RELATIONS

Founded in 1921, the Council on Foreign Relations is an independent, national membership organization and a nonpartisan center for scholars dedicated to producing and disseminating ideas so that individual and corporate members, as well as policymakers, journalists, students, and interested citizens in the United States and other countries, can better understand the world and the foreign policy choices facing the United States and other governments. The Council does this by convening meetings; conducting a wide-ranging Studies program; publishing *Foreign Affairs*, the preeminent journal covering international affairs and U.S. foreign policy; maintaining a diverse membership; sponsoring Independent Task Forces and Special Reports; and providing up-to-date information about the world and U.S. foreign policy on the Council's website, www.cfr.org.

THE COUNCIL TAKES NO INSTITUTIONAL POSITION ON POLICY ISSUES AND HAS NO AFFILIATION WITH THE U.S. GOVERNMENT. ALL STATEMENTS OF FACT AND EXPRESSIONS OF OPINION CONTAINED IN ITS PUBLICATIONS ARE THE SOLE RESPONSIBILITY OF THE AUTHOR OR AUTHORS.

Council Special Reports (CSRs) are concise policy briefs, produced to provide a rapid response to a developing crisis or contribute to the public's understanding of current policy dilemmas. CSRs are written by individual authors—who may be Council fellows or acknowledged experts from outside the institution—in consultation with an advisory committee, and typically take sixty days or less from inception to publication. The committee serves as a sounding board and provides feedback on a draft report. It usually meets twice—once before a draft is written and once again when there is a draft for review; however, advisory committee members, unlike Task Force members, are not asked to sign off on the report or to otherwise endorse it. Once published, CSRs are posted on the Council's website.

For further information about the Council or this Special Report, please write to the Council on Foreign Relations, 58 East 68th Street, New York, NY 10021, or call the Communications office at 212-434-9400. Visit our website at www.cfr.org.

CONTENTS

FOREWORD

The recent Dubai Ports World controversy has highlighted the extent to which America's critical infrastructure is not only largely in the hands of private companies, but that private sector ownership does not stop at the water's edge. This fact of twenty-first-century life makes all the more complex the task of securing the modern foundations upon which we depend. Americans must also be mindful of the reality that our energy, financial, information technology, food supply, transportation, and logistics sectors are interconnected with global systems. Safeguarding so many of the things that Americans depend upon is both a domestic and global challenge.

In this Council Special Report, Stephen E. Flynn and Daniel B. Prieto argue that there has been too little attention paid to the issue of critical infrastructure protection. They did not reach this conclusion by cloistering themselves in an ivory tower. Instead, they benefited from the experience and practical insights of a group of private sector leaders in the Council's Corporate membership. Over the course of one year, this group met with leading national experts on trade security, global disease, terrorism, risk management, emergency preparedness, and energy.

Now, well into our fifth year since the September 11, 2001, terrorist attacks on New York and Washington, DC, federal efforts to enlist the private sector in bolstering the security and resilience of vital modern systems remain largely stillborn. This report offers thoughtful and tightly reasoned analysis of why that is so. It proposes a new set of principles for advancing public-private partnerships to tackle this important agenda. Finally, it outlines some practical recommendations for how we can move quickly from where we are to where we need to be. The capabilities and civic-mindedness of our private sector is a national asset. The White House and Congress need to make capitalizing on that asset a top priority.

Richard N. Haass
President
Council on Foreign Relations
March 2006

v

ACKNOWLEDGMENTS

In January 2005, the Council on Foreign Relations initiated a year-long project, informed by a nonpartisan working group drawn entirely from the private sector, to assess the extent to which private entities are succeeding at making America safer. This was an extraordinary group of individuals who gave generously of their intellects, professional expertise, and time, participating in a series of working sessions and commenting on several drafts of this report. They are listed individually in the appendix and we are grateful to them all. We are particularly indebted to David Kellogg, Jacqui Schein, and Jana Gasn of the Council's Corporate Program for their great work in helping to identify and recruit these outstanding private sector leaders.

The project benefited from the participation of the nation's leading experts on trade security, global disease, terrorism, risk management, emergency preparedness, and energy. Over a series of seven sessions Robert C. Bonner, Laurie Garrett, Richard A. Clarke, Howard Kunreuther, Charles D. Ferguson, Joseph Pfeifer, and Daniel H. Yergin addressed our group. Thanks to their presentations, we all came away far wiser.

In capturing the findings and preparing meeting summaries, we were most ably assisted by Marcio Siwi, Sean Burke, Andrea M. Walther, and Robert Knake. Andrea M. Walther was the lead researcher for the project, tracking down most of the sources used in preparation of this report. Sean Burke and Rob Knake helped to prepare some of the first draft. We are indebted to Council President Richard N. Haass and Director of Studies James M. Lindsay for their valuable comments on the final draft. Lisa Shields and the Council's Communications department as well as Michelle Baute worked closely with us to develop an active outreach program. Patricia Dorff and Molly Graham in the Publications department provided crucial assistance in the production of this document.

The conclusions and recommendations contained in this report have been drawn from the input of the working group, but the final product reflects the views and summary judgments of its authors, who are responsible for any of its shortcomings.

Stephen E. Flynn
Daniel B. Prieto

EXECUTIVE SUMMARY

In policy and strategy documents since September 11, 2001, the Bush administration and Congress have repeatedly stressed the critical importance of "public-private partnerships" to make the country safer. Yet the capabilities, assets, and goodwill of the private sector to bolster our homeland security remain largely untapped. That is the primary conclusion reached by the Council on Foreign Relations working group on homeland security and the private sector over the course of one year.

This report identifies a way forward for public-private partnership on homeland security. It begins by laying out the policy dilemma in detail, offers a recent history of the security role of the private sector, highlights specific problems that have kept the public-private relationship from maturing, and offers a series of principles for a more productive relationship. It concludes with a series of specific recommendations—some will be the work of Congress, others the purview of the administration, still others the responsibility of the private sector—to secure the homeland better.

The federal government has largely taken a hands-off approach to the private sector, believing that market mechanisms will provide levels of security sufficient to address the modern terrorist threat. That belief has proven to be unfounded. The federal government must abandon its passive role and lead a truly collaborative effort to protect our national assets and leverage private sector capabilities in defense of the homeland.

Too many barriers remain for effective public-private coordination. Foremost among these is a lack of a reliable public partner for the private sector. The U.S. Department of Homeland Security (DHS) continues to struggle with growing pains. Nonetheless, the department leadership has taken certain steps that indicate a keener understanding of the private sector and the role it can play in securing the homeland. Chief among these is the use of risk-based criteria in Homeland Security Presidential Directive 7 (HSPD-7) to determine the priority for securing critical infrastructure. The National Response Plan (NRP) acknowledges the important role of the private sector in the management of high-consequence events. The private sector's response to Hurricanes Katrina and Rita showed what it is capable of during national calamities. However, these largely self-initiated efforts also showed that the federal government had little effective interface with the private sector to coordinate and manage the response and that the NRP suffers from significant flaws.

Given the evolving policy framework and ongoing organizational change within the federal government, it is important to note where we are in our efforts to establish effective public-private partnerships as the basis for laying a course to improve them. This report highlights the facts that are shaping the current policy dilemma and must be dealt with in any effective strategy for public-private partnership. These include the following:

- The federal government has failed to establish national priorities for critical infrastructure protection.
- The federal reorganization since 9/11 has raised the difficulty and transaction costs for the private sector to work with the federal government.
- Information sharing between government and the private sector remains stunted.
- Overall investment in private sector security initiatives has been modest.
- Private sector protective efforts have been more effective in sectors that face regular threats of criminal attack and in sectors that already must comply with established security regulations.
- The federal government has failed to provide meaningful incentives or standards for securing critical sectors that pose the highest risk and where voluntary efforts have proven to be insufficient.
- The private sector has not been effectively integrated into response and recovery planning for major disasters, though some promising public-private initiatives have been piloted.
- The federal government has not adequately developed alternatives to shutting down entire economic sectors in the aftermath of a terrorist attack, nor has it done sufficient planning for reopening these sectors.
- Insurance adoption has been promising, but it requires continued government engagement in the insurance market to be sustained.

In fixing these problems, Congress and the administration should bear in mind a few essential principles that can be used to identify what responsibilities should be met by the private sector, those that are the responsibility of government, and those that can be shared jointly. Policymakers should remember that the government is inevitably a major market player whose actions directly affect the ability of the private sector to invest more in security. For its part, the private sector is not just a target, but also an important source for information, assets, and capabilities that the government does not possess. Furthermore, policymakers should not overlook the fact that industry leaders possess a sense of patriotism and civic duty that can be harnessed to improve U.S. security. American companies are willing to commit their time, expertise, and resources to support the homeland security mission. The federal government must make a concerted effort to recognize and encourage such actions as part of a successful partnership between the federal government and the private sector.

Federal security efforts must be tailored to address specific vulnerabilities in individual sectors. Too often federal officials treat the private sector as if it were a single actor, yet the consequences of a terrorist attack on a critical sector vary widely by sector. The nature of the threat associated with attacks on each sector as well as sector-specific business constraints should inform the security measures taken to prevent an attack or mitigate its consequences. Some critical sectors are well prepared, while preparation in others remains poor. In setting priorities, the federal government should not only look at what industries would produce the greatest harm to society if struck. The government should also focus its efforts on those industries where there is the greatest gap between consequences and the current state of preparedness to prevent and recover quickly from attack should prevention measures fail.

In many industries, threat perceptions and conducive market conditions have resulted in adequate voluntary investments in security. In industries in which voluntary investment has been insufficient, government intervention is necessary and desirable. Nonregulatory approaches are often preferable, but when voluntary efforts do not achieve adequate levels of security, lawmakers and regulators may need to take action. Furthermore, Washington must realize that government regulation is not always in conflict with the best interests of the private sector. In many instances, federal action can help to bound market uncertainties, making it easier for markets to work and for the private sector to make investment decisions. For example, by helping establish and enforce uniform standards, the federal government can provide a predictable environment that will better allow companies to invest in security without fear that such efforts will be undercut by competitors that do not follow suit, or that investments will be rendered obsolete because the government later ends up standardizing a different set of technologies or practices. Federal standards would also help ease industry fears of liability should their security efforts be defeated by a terrorist attack.

To make America more secure, the federal government urgently needs to provide better leadership on homeland security issues and become an active partner with the private sector on target protection, preparedness, response, and recovery.

1. Washington needs to change its policy paradigm regarding the private sector, which, in effect, tells companies to protect themselves. On critical infrastructure issues, Washington needs to provide leadership, not followership.

2. Either DHS or a group of outside experts needs to quickly complete, as required by law, a national list of priorities for critical infrastructure that can serve as a strategic road map for spending and protective actions. At the same time, Washington should not allow completion of this list to delay immediate efforts to improve security where well-known and widely acknowledged security gaps exist.

3. Washington must move beyond talking about the need to dramatically improve information sharing with the private sector and hold government officials accountable for actually doing it.

4. DHS must strengthen the quality and experience of its personnel. One way to do this would be to establish a personnel exchange program with the private sector.

5. Congress and the administration should work closely with industry to establish security standards and implement and enforce regulations where necessary and, especially, where industry is seeking standards and regulation.

6. Congress should establish targeted tax incentives to promote investments in security and resiliency in the highest-risk industries.

7. Congress should establish federal liability protections for companies that undertake meaningful security improvements.

8. Homeland security officials should substantially increase the number of exercises for responding to catastrophic events. Private sector assets and capabilities should be fully integrated into these exercises, with a view to achieving deeper private sector integration into national and regional emergency response plans.

9. Federal response plans should identify specialized supplies/capabilities that will be in short supply following certain types of terrorist incidents or high-consequence events, including vaccines, ventilators, electric transformers, laboratory capacity, and decontamination equipment. Washington should work with the private sector to ensure the availability of these supplies and capabilities.

10. DHS should establish a federal awards program, modeled after the prestigious Malcolm Baldridge National Quality Awards program, which recognizes private sector achievement and innovation in homeland security.

INTRODUCTION

Since 9/11, the Bush administration and Congress have called for a public-private partnership to improve homeland security. In January 2005, the Council on Foreign Relations initiated a yearlong project, informed by a nonpartisan working group drawn entirely from the private sector, to assess the extent to which private entities are succeeding at making America safer. The recommendations and conclusions contained in this report have been drawn from the input of the working group, informed by a series of meetings with respected experts on bioterrorism, cybersecurity, insurance, trade and transportation security, energy, and emergency preparedness. The working group sought to identify strategic issues that transcend specific sectors and to formulate broad policy recommendations to improve industry-government partnership on homeland security issues. Our conclusion is that the federal government is not doing nearly enough to harness the capabilities, assets, and goodwill of the private sector to bolster our national state of preparedness.

The 9/11 terrorist attacks fundamentally altered the security roles and responsibilities of the private sector. The use of commercial aircraft as missiles against the World Trade Center and the Pentagon, and a steady stream of statements by al-Qaeda leaders declaring their intention to "fill [American] hearts with terror and target [America's] economic lifeline," have made it clear that the critical infrastructures that support our society and economy—including transportation, oil and gas, electricity, water, chemicals, telecommunications, computers, and the food supply—are likely targets of future terrorist attacks. Because the vast majority of that infrastructure is owned and/or operated by the private sector, America's businesses must be part of any national effort to confront the threat of catastrophic terrorism.

While the current national homeland security strategy rightly recognizes the critical homeland security role of the private sector, since 9/11 federal policy and practice has abdicated too much of the government's constitutional obligation "to provide for the common defense" and "to promote the general welfare." Beyond law enforcement and military efforts to detect and intercept or attack terrorists before they strike, Washington's homeland security policies place too great an expectation for safeguarding the most valuable and vulnerable civilian targets within America's borders on the private sector.[1] The White House and Congress wrongly presume that market mechanisms on their own will provide sufficient incentives to provide the necessary level of security in the absence of decisive federal leadership and involvement.

There are three straightforward reasons why relying on the market as the primary catalyst for critical infrastructure protection is flawed. First—as Adam Smith pointed out more than two centuries ago in his landmark treatise, *The Wealth of Nations*—security is a public good and a core responsibility of the government. The electorate ultimately and rightly holds political leaders responsible for providing it. Second, by relegating to itself the limited role of "protector of last resort"—a backstop only for those areas that fall through the private sector cracks—Washington ends up taking a wait-and-see approach that both delays the pursuit of practical security measures and diminishes a much needed sense of urgency. Third, when it is *assumed* that the private sector is prepared and secure, the only way to validate whether companies have really done enough is after terrorists strike. If the attack involves a weapon of mass destruction (WMD) or has WMD-like effects, discovering after the fact that too little was done by private actors is simply an unacceptable way to protect the interests of the public.

While there are practical barriers to having the private sector assume the bulk of the responsibility for the post-9/11 security mandate, leaving it to the government alone to map the path ahead is not a workable alternative. When the government announces requirements or "best practices" after lengthy deliberative processes and usually with nominal industry input, it almost always misses the mark. More often than not, the proposed or mandated safeguards reflect a poor understanding of the design and operation of critical infrastructures, the business constraints that face owners of critical infrastructure, the substantial diversity within the private sector, and the real versus

---

[1] Office of Homeland Security, White House, *National Strategy for Homeland Security*, July 16, 2002, which assigns most of the responsibility for funding the protection of potential targets within U.S. borders to the private sector. It lays out "the broad principles that should guide the allocation of funding for homeland security [and] help determine who should bear the financial burdens" and states that "the government should only address those activities that the market does not adequately provide—for example, national defense or border security....For other aspects of homeland security, sufficient incentives exist in the private market to supply protection. In these cases we should rely on the private sector." See http://www.whitehouse.gov/homeland/book/nat_strat_hls.pdf.

perceived vulnerabilities. That is because many of the most critical issues span multiple agency jurisdictions and these agencies rarely work well together. The results end up being a mix of unacknowledged gaps and misguided or redundant requirements.

The impasse boils down to this: The design, ownership, and day-to-day operational knowledge of many of the nation's most essential systems rest almost exclusively with the private sector. But security and safety are public goods whose provision is a core responsibility of government at all levels. The government is unable to protect things about which it has only a peripheral understanding and over which it has a limited jurisdictional reach; and the market is unlikely to provide the socially desirable level of security. Private companies generally will pursue investments that make sense for their core businesses and offer greater returns than alternative investments. Even when companies do make additional security investments in the interest of patriotism or good corporate citizenship, as many companies have done since 9/11, those efforts may not be sufficient, and such efforts will not be sustained if they produce a cost disadvantage or increase liability exposure relative to competitors that decide not to make similar security investments.

The federal government must abandon its essentially passive support role and, instead, lead a truly collaborative national effort to leverage extensive private sector capabilities and assets for protecting against, responding to, and recovering from high-consequence events, including terrorism and natural disasters. Historically, America's private sector has shown itself to be a willing security partner. That was certainly the case during World War II, when the full energy of the private sector was harnessed to provide "the Arsenal of Democracy." In more recent times, company executives continue to demonstrate their willingness to look beyond their bottom-line interests to provide their ingenuity and resources to support the nation in times of crisis. For instance, in the immediate aftermath of 9/11, Target Corporation, General Motors, and other members of the U.S. Department of the Treasury's Commercial Operations Advisory Committee led an effort to help develop a new protocol for advancing trade security that has became the Customs-Trade Partnership Against Terrorism (C-TPAT). The program has not yet led to an effective regime of secure inspection and reliable movement of goods equal to the terrorist threat. However, it has enlisted 5,800 companies seeking to work with the government to improve security and customs together.

In response to Hurricanes Katrina and Rita, companies like Wal-Mart and Home Depot proved far more nimble at providing manpower, materials, and logistics than many parts of the federal government. While truckloads of ice contracted by the Federal Emergency Management Agency (FEMA) were stranded for days with no direction on where to go, national retailers were organizing important distribution points for food, water, clothing, generators, and other supplies. Mississippi Power, a subsidiary of Southern Company, was able to restore electricity to hundreds of thousands of customers well ahead of schedule. The security services company Guardsmark tracked down all of its missing employees who lived and worked in the storm-struck area within a week and provided them with cash, emergency supplies, and help with relocation. Johnson Controls bought recreational vehicles in Wisconsin and shipped them to campgrounds in the disaster zone so its employees had temporary housing. Even though Katrina and Rita were natural disasters as opposed to man-made ones, they illustrate that the nation will be far better served when the federal government is organized to fully integrate the private sector as a partner in preventing and responding to catastrophic terrorist attacks.

Unfortunately, too many barriers remain for the private sector to cooperate fully with government entities to enhance homeland security. First, the public sector is still not organized to be an effective partner. The Department of Homeland Security is struggling to fulfill the lofty expectations that accompanied its creation after 9/11. It suffers from high management turnover and inadequate staffing. DHS's own employees recently rated it at or near the bottom of the entire federal government for adequacy of resources, quality of management, accountability, and creativity and innovation.[2] Making matters worse, unresolved conflicts over agency jurisdiction persist, and bureaucratic hesitancy to take on new responsibilities in the absence of additional resources to do the job prevails. Moreover, there exists an enduring legacy of an often-adversarial relationship between the private sector and government stemming from government's regulatory oversight and

---

[2] U.S. Office of Personnel Management, *Federal Human Capital Survey 2004,* see http://www.fhcs2004. opm.gov/. For analysis of results related to DHS, see Scott Lilly, *An Analysis of Employee Attitudes at Federal Departments and Federal Agencies: What a Recent Government Survey Tells Us About Our Efforts to Protect Ourselves Against Terrorist Attacks and Respond to Natural Disasters* (Washington, DC: Center for American Progress, October 17, 2005).

enforcement roles. Further, many of the structures in place, such as the laws and regulations that guide the interaction within and among these sectors, remain unchanged to address the imperatives of 9/11. For instance, antitrust laws put severe constraints on the ability of industry leaders to come together and agree on common protocols. Also, companies that make a good-faith effort to undertake antiterrorist measures potentially risk open-ended liability issues should terrorists succeed at defeating those measures. Only government can create the legal mechanisms to place limits on liability.

In short, we cannot proceed from where we are to where we must be unless there is far more public-private cooperation than now exists. That will require deciding which critical infrastructure sectors pose the most serious unaddressed security risks and setting priorities accordingly. Policies and programs must achieve better information sharing, provide targeted incentives to encourage greater security investments in the riskiest industries, establish liability protections that give industry credit for undertaking good-faith security measures, improve the availability of commercial insurance and security-audit products, and better integrate the private sector with all levels of government in response and recovery planning. The roles and responsibilities of the component agencies within DHS need to be delineated better, which will reduce the confusion experienced by private companies when dealing with the department. Jurisdictional lines between DHS, Federal Bureau of Investigation (FBI), and other regulatory agencies involved in critical infrastructure protection must also be more clearly defined. Finally, Congress and the administration must be willing to consider appropriate regulation when the market is unable to put in place adequate security measures on its own.

Closer collaboration between the federal government and the private sector to address the threat of terrorism will make the nation more secure. It also will reduce the likelihood that the government, in an overreaction to future terrorist attacks, implements poorly informed or draconian policies that needlessly create additional harm.

THE SECURITY ROLE OF THE PRIVATE SECTOR:
POLICY EVOLUTION AND RECENT HISTORY

The emphasis Washington has placed on the security role of the private sector actually began prior to 9/11. In 1997, President Bill Clinton created the Commission on Critical Infrastructure Protection to address vulnerabilities in important sectors in the U.S. economy stemming from the increasing interdependence and reliance on information technology. The commission stressed the importance of mobilizing the private sector as part of a national effort to address the growing vulnerability of these "critical infrastructures" on which the nation's health, welfare, and security relied.

The terrorist attacks on New York and Washington refocused the attention of policymakers on the vulnerability of private sector assets. Policy reforms regarding critical infrastructure and information sharing were established in the Patriot Act, the Homeland Security Act, presidential directives and executive orders, and White House strategy documents. New organizations, programs, and activities were established, especially within the newly formed Department of Homeland Security, to deal specifically with the private sector on critical infrastructure and information sharing.

Despite acknowledging the importance of critical infrastructure protection as well as asserting the critical need for "public-private partnerships," the White House homeland security strategy assigned the federal government an essentially passive role when it comes to protecting potential targets within U.S. borders:

> The government should only address those activities that the market does not adequately provide—for example, national defense or border security.... For other aspects of homeland security, sufficient incentives exist in the private market to supply protection. In these cases we should rely on the private sector.[3]

This policy assumption has had far-reaching implications for the efficacy of critical infrastructure protection and efforts to establish meaningful public-private

---

[3] Office of Homeland Security, White House, *National Strategy for Homeland Security*, July 16, 2002.

cooperation on homeland security. These implications are analyzed at length later in this report.

Over the past two years, in part due to federal budget pressures and critical assessments of DHS's effectiveness, the federal government has moved toward a more risk-based approach to homeland security. Homeland Security Presidential Directive 7, in December 2003, for the first time placed a relative priority on critical infrastructures based on severity of consequences. In particular, it assigned priority to infrastructures that if attacked could have significant health or casualty effects "comparable to those from the use of a weapon of mass destruction" or could threaten the overall economy, either directly or through cascading impacts on other sectors. Homeland Security Secretary Michael Chertoff has made prioritizing protective activities and funding on a risk basis a top goal for his department since taking office in February 2005. Congress has indicated moves in that direction as well, but will continue to struggle with those efforts because America continues to lack clear homeland security strategic priorities and a comprehensive national risk analysis. In early 2006, DHS for the first time began allocating a portion of homeland security grant funding to states on the basis of risk.

Policies regarding the private sector's role in homeland security evolved further with the December 2004 National Response Plan. The NRP acknowledged the important role of the private sector in the management of domestic high-consequence events, including terrorism and natural disasters. However, the NRP focused primarily on providing direction for the federal government's disaster response and largely overlooked the need to engage actively the private sector in *advance* of a serious domestic incident. Hurricanes Katrina and Rita exposed this and other significant weaknesses with the NRP while highlighting the limits in federal capabilities to respond to high-consequence events.[4] At the same time, the important role played by the private sector in response to recent hurricanes demonstrated the largely untapped potential of private companies to provide services, material, logistics, and other capabilities. Better advance integration of the private sector into planning, preparedness, response, and recovery is the next logical evolution of federal homeland security policy and public-private partnerships.

---

[4] White House, *The Federal Response to Hurricane Katrina: Lessons Learned,* Washington, DC, February 2006, see http://www.whitehouse.gov/reports/katrina-lessons-learned.pdf.

THE PRIVATE SECTOR AND HOMELAND SECURITY:
A PROGRESS REPORT

In light of the evolving policy framework and significant organizational changes following 9/11, it is appropriate to take stock of where things stand today on critical infrastructure protection and establishing public-private partnerships for homeland security.

FEDERAL PRIORITIES FOR CRITICAL INFRASTRUCTURES

The federal government still has failed to establish priorities for critical infrastructure protection.

The Homeland Security Act of 2002 requires DHS to assess comprehensively critical infrastructure vulnerabilities, prioritize protective measures, develop a comprehensive national plan, and craft policies for securing those infrastructures. Furthermore, the *National Strategy for the Physical Protection of Critical Infrastructures and Key Assets* calls for DHS to identify critical infrastructure-protection priorities. These requirements have not been completed. As recently as November 2005, the government's infrastructure-protection plans continue to discuss the *process* by which priorities and protective actions will be developed, acknowledging that priorities still do not exist.[5]

More than four years after 9/11, the United States should be well beyond talking about how to develop priorities. These should have been decided long ago, and protective measures should be well under way. While a comprehensive risk analysis should be undertaken, there are critical infrastructure sectors that are widely recognized as posing significant risks to the nation: chemical facilities near urban population centers have the potential to inflict the greatest casualties; attacks on the electric grid, oil and gas facilities, and major ports have the potential to create the greatest cascading economic effects; and

---

[5] Department of Homeland Security, *Draft National Infrastructure Protection Plan (NIPP) Base Plan*, November 2, 2005, pp. 36 and 89, see http://www.fas.org/irp/agency/dhs/nipp110205.pdf.

for sheer ease of targeting and based on historic frequency of attacks, ground transportation targets face the most likely threat.[6]

DHS efforts to develop critical infrastructure priorities have relied significantly on asset lists submitted by states in the run-up to the Iraq War. That approach failed to incorporate a systematic national evaluation that weighed the relative risks across states. Furthermore, this bottom-up approach neglected to leverage the vast technical expertise available from critical infrastructure companies, world-class U.S. consulting firms, and leading academic and research institutions, such as the National Academies of Sciences.

GOVERNMENT AS A PARTNER

In the near term, the massive federal reorganization since 9/11 has raised the difficulty and transaction costs for the private sector to work with the federal government.

Private companies continue to face a dynamic and unsettled bureaucratic landscape. The widely documented challenges associated with starting up the Department of Homeland Security, delineating new lines of authority across the federal government, and building expertise and continuity in the face of high turnover among personnel and a high reliance on contractors and civil servants who are only on temporary assignments to the department have led most private companies to adopt a "wait-and-see" approach to homeland security.

Companies are frustrated further by jurisdictional overlap within DHS and the persistence of blurred lines of authority and accountability in many areas that involve

---

[6] On chemicals, see Thomas J. Ridge and Christine Todd Whitman, "Letter to the Editor," *Washington Post*, October 6, 2002, p. B6. On the electric grid, see Paul H. Gilbert, *Implications of Power Blackouts for the Nation's Cybersecurity and Critical Infrastructure Protection*, National Research Council, testimony before the Joint Hearing of the Subcommittee on Cybersecurity, Science, and Research and Development and the Subcommittee on Infrastructure and Border Security, Select Committee on Homeland Security House of Representatives, 108th Congress, September 4, 2003. On oil and gas, see Hassan M. Fattah, "Attack on Saudi Oil Facility Thwarted," *New York Times*, February 24, 2006, available at http://www.nytimes.com/2006/02/24/international/middleeast/24cnd-saudi.html?ex=1298437200&en=76 380289e5cc27f8&ei=5088&partner=rssnyt&emc=rss. On ports, see Stephen E. Flynn, *America the Vulnerable* (New York: HarperCollins, 2004). On ground transport, see Daniel B. Prieto, *Mass Transit Security After the London Bombings*, testimony before the Commonwealth of Massachusetts Joint Committee on Public Safety and Homeland Security, August 4, 2005, available at http://bcsia.ksg. harvard.edu/publication.cfm?program=CORE&ctype=testimony&item_id=50.

federal departments outside of DHS. Unclear lines of authority mean that too often private sector security issues fall into gaps between agencies or gaps created by DHS's immaturity, disarray, and lack of bureaucratic stature relative to other agencies. At the other extreme, when the federal government does engage the private sector, lack of intra-agency coordination means companies too often face duplicative and sometimes conflicting threat information and requests for information. Ongoing turf issues among congressional committees only compound the challenge of working with Washington on homeland security matters.[7]

INFORMATION SHARING

Information sharing between government and the private sector remains stunted.[8] Government agencies find it difficult to share anything but the most general threat information with private companies out of fear that it will be leaked or that intelligence sources and methods will be compromised. Companies worry about possible liability issues or being placed at a competitive disadvantage should information they disclose to government authorities not be properly protected. The roles and responsibilities for information sharing remain largely unclear. The consensus among corporate security officers is that information sharing with federal law enforcement officials is too often a one-way street (i.e., companies provide specific information when appropriate but receive little information of value in return from the government). Lacking sufficient access to reliable threat information, companies find it difficult to make informed cost-benefit decisions that might justify greater security investments. For insurance companies, lack of better threat information makes it difficult to price terrorism insurance policies to

---

[7] Business Executives for National Security (BENS) and the Center for Strategic and International Studies (CSIS), *Untangling the Web: Congressional Oversight and the Department of Homeland Security,* Washington, DC, December 2004, see http://www.bens.org/White%20Paper_Final.pdf; 9/11 Public Discourse Project, *Final Report on 9/11 Commission Recommendation,* December 5, 2005, see http://www.9-11pdp.org/press/2005-12-05_report.pdf.

[8] For an in-depth discussion of information sharing with the private sector, see Daniel B. Prieto, "Information Sharing with the Private Sector: History, Challenges, Innovation, and Prospects," in Philip Auerswald, Lewis M. Branscomb, Todd M. La Porte, and Erwann Michel-Kerjan, eds., *Seeds of Disaster, Roots of Response: How Private Action Can Reduce Public Vulnerability* (Cambridge, England: Cambridge University Press, forthcoming).

accurately reflect risk. That fact in turn deprives the market of an important transmission mechanism to convey signals that might cause companies to increase investments in security in order to get discounts on their insurance premiums. Without a clear sense of both the probability and character of potential threats, making practical decisions about investing in countermeasures becomes little better than guesswork. A shortage of experienced personnel with relevant industry experience or knowledge within DHS and elsewhere across the federal government also contributes to the difficulty in improving information sharing with the private sector. The Private Sector Office within the DHS, while helpful as a starting point, has largely served as a liaison and outreach office with no operational responsibilities. The private sector receives threat information from multiple government channels, which often are not coordinated and may conflict. For example, the FBI and DHS have demonstrated a lack of coordination on the release of threat information regarding the financial sector, oil refineries, and mass transit.[9]

PRIVATE SECTOR INVESTMENT IN SECURITY

Overall investment in private sector security initiatives has been modest.
Despite declaratory goals embedded in federal policy and increased awareness of the issue among private sector executives, since 9/11, "relatively little additional [security] spending has come from the private sector."[10] For the first few years following 9/11, surveys indicate that the private sector had increased its spending on security by only 3–4 percent per year.[11]

While more spending by the private sector on security is a step in the right direction, there remain substantial shortfalls in the level of security investment in the sectors most at risk. That gap stems from the public-goods nature of security; business,

---

[9] Thomas Frank, "Terror Warning Surprises Homeland Security Department," *Newsday*, May 28, 2004; Chris Strohm, "Threat Warning Creates Confusion Over Homeland Security Roles," GovExec.com; John Mintz and Susan Schmidt, "Ashcroft Assailed on Terror Warning," *Washington Post*, May 28, 2004, p. A4; Mark Sherman, "Subway Threat Puzzle: When Local Officials, Feds Disagree," *Associated Press*, October 7, 2005; and Leonard Leavitt, "NYPD's Voice Loud and Clear," *Newsday*, October 14, 2005.

[10] Congressional Budget Office, *Homeland Security and the Private Sector*, December 2004.

[11] See Conference Board, *Corporate Security Management: Organization and Spending Since 9/11*, New York, July 2003.

economic, and information constraints faced by individual companies; and a lack of decisive leadership by federal authorities.

PRIVATE SECTOR PROTECTIVE EFFORTS

Private sector protective efforts have been more effective in sectors that face regular threats of criminal attack and in sectors that already must comply with established security regulations.

Finance and information technology (IT) companies generally are well prepared against cyberthreats. The companies' level of preparedness stems not from government regulations, but because they face criminal threats of fraud and hacking on a daily basis, and those threats place at risk core assets that generate revenues and profits for their businesses. Finance and IT companies are also well positioned to make investments that address cyberthreats because their business models provide the growth and profitability to fund these investments and because capital assets like computer systems and software are upgraded with relative frequency. This quick capital turnover gives these companies frequent opportunities to implement up-to-date security solutions within the normal course of business. A failure to invest adequately in security would put finance and IT companies at a competitive disadvantage. Regulations in this instance likely would interfere with adequate private sector security efforts. They would likely be redundant or quickly outmoded, as the time it takes to craft new standards would not keep up with the pace of rapidly changing IT.

At the other extreme, industries like commercial aviation and nuclear power that are regulated at the federal level are making better progress on security than are sectors that have historically been regulated primarily at the state and local levels. When federal regulators exercise close oversight, it can create tension between the private sector and the government. At the same time, though, regulators end up acquiring a greater familiarity with the operations of the sector in question and also end up forging formal and informal relationships with the private sector to manage issues as they arise. Industry knowledge and individual relationships have proven helpful in developing and speeding the rate of adoption of new industry-wide security standards, as has been the case at commercial airports. Meanwhile, progress in bolstering security within the surface and mass transit transportation sectors, where there are no counterparts analogous to the Federal Aviation Administration (FAA) and Transportation Security Administration (TSA), have lagged behind. Similarly, the Nuclear Regulatory Commission (NRC) has always required that nuclear facilities be designed from the outset to be hardened and secure, and that armed security forces be on-site to defend against armed attacks.[12] After 9/11, the NRC was able to quickly add a host of new security requirements that are now largely in place.[13] But little progress has been made in improving security of the electrical distribution system, which has historically received little in the way of federal oversight.

INCENTIVES AND STANDARDS

Since 9/11, the federal government has failed to provide meaningful incentives or standards for securing critical sectors that pose the highest risk and where voluntary efforts have proven to be insufficient.

Chemical facilities, especially those near urban population centers, remain among the most dangerous of potential critical infrastructure targets in the United States.[14] The fact that they remain potentially deadly targets stems from several factors. First, chemical companies have not yet faced direct attacks on their infrastructure, so it is more difficult to put together the business case for new security measures. Second, the long life and

---

[12] Nuclear Energy Institute, *CSIS "Silent Vector" Energy Terrorism Exercise Finds Nuclear Power Plants "Best Defended Targets,"* press release, October 21, 2002, see http://www.nei.org/index.asp? catnum=3&catid=959.

[13] See U.S. Nuclear Regulatory Commission, *NRC Approves Changes to the Design Basis Threat and Issues Orders for Nuclear Power Plants to Further Enhance Security*, press release, April 29, 2003, see http://www.nrc.gov/reading-rm/doc-collections/news/2003/03-053.html.

[14] Robert Block, "Chemical Plants Still Have Few Terror Controls," *Wall Street Journal*, August 20, 2004, p. B1; and Richard A. Falkenrath, *Chemical Attack on America: How Vulnerable Are We?* panel 2, testimony before the U.S. Senate Committee on Homeland Security and Governmental Affairs, April 27, 2005, p. 10, see http://hsgac.senate.gov/_files/SHSGACTestimonyonHazmat042705.pdf. "In short, the casualty potential of a terrorist attack against a large TIH [toxic inhalation hazard] chemical container near a population center is comparable to that of a fully successful terrorist employment of an improvised nuclear device or effective biological weapon. The difference is that TIH chemical containers are substantially easier to attack than improvised nuclear devices or effective biological weapon are to acquire or fabricate."

substantial upfront cost of chemical manufacturing facilities means that security-related capital improvements like facilities redesign and retrofits would be costly and will occur infrequently, even if these companies were to include such security upgrades in the normal cycle of capital expenditures. Third, making significant security investments has the potential to put a company at a competitive disadvantage if industry competitors do not follow suit, and if the costs of security upgrades are not readily offset or recoverable, for example, in the form of reduced insurance premiums.

While leading chemical companies have voluntarily spent close to $3 billion since 9/11 to enhance security, many facilities still remain vulnerable to an attack carried out by determined terrorists.[15] Additionally, the companies that are increasing security spending are being placed at a competitive disadvantage relative to companies making little to no new security investments. These factors have led the American Chemistry Council, which represents companies responsible for roughly 90 percent of U.S. commercial chemical production but that account for less than 15 percent of U.S. facilities that handle or store significant quantities of hazardous chemicals, to ask the federal government to step in with security regulations and stronger government oversight and enforcement.[16] To date, the government has been resistant to doing so. In addition, as a former senior White House homeland security official recently testified, "[the] administration has not exercised its authority to enhance the security of toxic chemicals in transit in any significant way since 9/11."[17] Regulation of chemical security is necessary, just as it has proven to be for the aviation and nuclear power industries.

Common regulations that are uniformly enforced are especially important in the transportation sector. Trains, trucks, planes, and ships almost always operate within and pass through multiple jurisdictions. Additionally, it is not possible to move cargo readily across different transportation modes unless standards are harmonized. If cargo

---

[15] Authors' email communication with James W. Conrad Jr., assistant general counsel, American Chemistry Council, February 9, 2006.

[16] Letter from the American Chemistry Council President and CEO, Jack N. Gerard, to Senator Susan Collins (R-ME), chair, Senate Committee on Homeland Security and Government Affairs, October 3, 2005; Jack N. Gerard, "Security Oversight Is Critical: Chemical-makers Took Safety Initiative. Now, Congress Must Act," *USA Today*, July 12, 2005, p. 10A.

[17] Richard A. Falkenrath, *Chemical Attack on America: How Vulnerable Are We?* panel two, testimony before the U.S. Senate Committee on Homeland Security and Governmental Affairs, April 27, 2005, p. 12.

containers came in many different sizes, they could not be easily transferred from a truck to a train to a ship as happens millions of times each day around the globe.

Recognizing both the need to enhance security and to develop workable and uniform standards for advancing it, the maritime industry willingly has supported pilot projects such as Operation Safe Commerce, the Safe and Secure Trade Corridor Initiative, and the Hong Kong Integrated Container Inspection System pilot. Yet none of these initiatives has led to new proposed standards by the Bush administration for bolstering container security. Maritime industry leaders have expressed frustration that, despite their investment in time, energy, and expense, there has been so little progress on this agenda. They have also made it clear that without the sustained engagement of the U.S. government, it simply will not be possible to forge the level of global cooperation required to address well-documented vulnerabilities.

RESPONSE AND RECOVERY

The private sector has not been effectively integrated into response and recovery planning for high-consequence events. A particularly urgent challenge is the need to ensure post-event surge capacity within the private sector. Some promising public-private initiatives have been piloted.

The National Response Plan is the federal blueprint for managing domestic disasters. While the NRP recognizes the importance of the private sector, the approach to engaging companies before and after catastrophes is ad hoc. One glaring shortfall has been the very limited integration of private sector entities in national homeland security exercises.

Treating the private sector as an afterthought in planning for high-consequence events makes little sense. If a terrorist attack were to occur during the daytime, the majority of adult Americans would be at work. Large employers have their own emergency and evacuation plans. The ability of corporations to provide instructions to tens of thousands of their own employees after a catastrophic event could be valuable in aiding government efforts to direct and organize a city's population after an event.

Private entities will also play an important role in mitigating the consequences of a catastrophic event, for example, shutting off gas lines to protect first responders as they battle fires, or accommodating spikes in communications traffic, or trying to restore basic services like power, water, communications, and transport.

Private companies are also adept at providing material, logistics, and know-how to provide relief in the aftermath of a disaster. For instance, private companies can marshal heavy-lifting equipment and cutting torches to assist in urban search and rescue. Pharmacies can provide essential health-care goods such as sterile bandages and antibiotics. Surge in demand for hospital beds and medical staff usually occurs through mutual aid agreements between private and public health-care facilities within a given geographic region.

However, there are some needs that the marketplace would not normally be able to meet without direct government intervention, such as the vaccine for smallpox. Since the disease has been effectively eradicated and routine vaccination has been stopped, the medical community no longer maintains a supply of the vaccine. If terrorists obtained the variola virus and used it as a bioterrorism agent to cause an outbreak, there would not be time to finance manufacturing the vaccine to protect the American people. Accordingly, it falls to the government to develop and to maintain stockpiles to confront this risk, which it has been doing under the Bioshield Act.

Another vulnerability that the market lacks an incentive to address is having enough spare electric transformers to support the smooth functioning of the U.S. power grid should several transformers be destroyed. High-voltage transformers can take many months to replace because relatively few are kept in inventory, they are custom-made to reflect the load requirements of individual utilities, they are very large (nearly half a million pounds) and difficult to transport, and they are costly (roughly $1 million each). Deregulated power companies have to worry about the effect on their bottom line of purchasing and maintaining a supply of spare transformers. But the absence of spare transformers could lead to lengthy regional blackouts should terrorists successfully attack electricity infrastructure, as they have done and become more adept at doing in Iraq since the U.S. invasion. The federal government should step in to ensure there is an adequate inventory of transformers on hand to address this vulnerability.

A promising public-private partnership called the New Jersey Business Force could serve as a model for the rest of the nation. Under that program, private sector companies have pledged resources (e.g., trucks, warehouses) to New Jersey during major disasters based on pre-identified needs. In addition, private sector volunteers have undergone training to administer vaccinations, support first responders, assist emergency professionals, and provide surge capacity manpower. Companies have also participated in exercises and training and have been integrated into the state's emergency response planning.

PLANNING FOR THE AFTERMATH OF A TERRORIST ATTACK

In the aftermath of a terrorist attack, the federal government has not developed adequate alternatives to shutting down entire essential sectors, nor has it done sufficient planning for reopening these sectors.

On 9/11, the response by the U.S. government was to ground all aviation for seventy-two hours until every aircraft could be checked to confirm that it did not pose a terrorist risk. Should there be a 9/11-style attack involving a maritime container, the response will likely be to close all U.S. ports until U.S. officials can confirm there is no risk of a follow-on attack. That is so even though the White House's September 2005 National Maritime Security Strategy calls for a more measured response. However, the administration has still not completed a recovery plan to guide government actions in the aftermath of an attack. As a result, reopening U.S. ports and restoring the flow of commercial traffic across U.S. borders is likely to take considerably more time than three days. In the interim, the global intermodal transportation system will grind to a virtual standstill, at a cost of at least $1 billion per day for the first seven days and additionally after that. Yet the federal government has not worked out a plan with the maritime industry and the international community on how to get the system moving again. Given the system's complexity, patching together new protocols in the aftermath of an incident will inevitably produce considerable confusion and unnecessary delays with all the attendant costs.

Similarly, should there be a bioterrorism incident in the food sector, there is no detailed plan of action to guide the response by industry, local, state, and federal agencies. The resources and authorities of state agencies vary considerably. At the federal level, the responsibility for food safety is divided between the U.S. Department of Agriculture and the Food and Drug Administration. As a result, a major disease outbreak could easily involve dozens of agencies with no one clearly in charge. Confusion over who has an obligation to file reports, who has jurisdiction, and just what the appropriate response should be to an agroterrorist attack will seriously compromise public confidence. This problem will be compounded by the fact that there is such limited capacity to conduct laboratory tests for exotic contaminants. Without testing, it would be impossible to quickly reassure an anxious public that food is safe, once a highly publicized incident takes place. As result, an agroterrorist incident that results in few actual casualties could still cause devastating economic consequences for large segments of the food industry.

GOVERNMENT ENGAGEMENT IN THE INSURANCE MARKET

Insurance adoption has been promising, but it requires continued government engagement in the insurance market to be sustained.

Terrorism risk differs from other insurable risks in a number of important ways. First, insurers lack sufficient actuarial data and are not privy to classified intelligence information that would allow them to assess the likelihood of terrorist events. That makes it difficult for them to set and adjust prices that accurately reflect risk. Second, terrorism risks are likely to be highly concentrated geographically or by industry, which increases the difficulty of creating a sufficiently large pool of insurers and reinsurers to spread the risk and make losses manageable. Third, the threat of natural disasters is an independent variable, effectively unaffected by government policy. Terrorist threats, on the other hand, can be influenced by actions taken by the U.S. government. For instance, when the United States was preparing to invade Iraq, the homeland security threat level was elevated because of a concern that the invasion might spawn terrorist attacks in response.

Policies and programs to harden one set of potential targets may encourage terrorists to shift their attention toward softer targets. Finally, when earthquakes or hurricanes strike, insurance policies generally do not seek to ascribe fault to a third party. But terrorist attacks can generate a flood of liability claims, as occurred in the immediate aftermath of the 9/11 attacks.

Because of the unique characteristics associated with terrorism risk, most industrialized countries have recognized the ongoing need for the government to be involved in the terrorism insurance market.[18] Following the 9/11 attacks, the U.S. Congress enacted the Terrorism Risk Insurance Act (TRIA) in 2002, which required insurance companies to make terrorism insurance available, but capped potential losses, after which federal assistance would become available. That intervention worked to stem the movement by insurers toward excluding terrorism from coverage. While the federal government requires that insurance coverage be available, it has not involved itself in setting the rates. The market has responded with reasonably priced terrorism insurance coverage that more and more private companies have been buying since 9/11. As of the end of 2004, 48 percent of commercial properties had purchased nonworkers' compensation terrorism insurance.[19] The subscription rates for these policies are the highest in the Northeast, where businesses and people are most densely populated and where the experience of the 9/11 attacks has sustained a sense of ongoing risk. The extension of TRIA in December 2005 has aided the continued development of the market for terrorism insurance.

---

[18] U.S. Government Accountability Office, *Catastrophe Risk: U.S. and European Approaches to Insure Natural Catastrophe and Terrorism Risks*, GAO-05-199, February 2005, see http://www.gao.gov/new. items/d05199.pdf.
[19] Marsh Inc. and the Insurance Information Institute, "Terrorism Insurance Market Overview: Terrorism Take-Up Rates, Coverage Types and Pricing," powerpoint presentation, February 2006.

GUIDING PRINCIPLES FOR ADVANCING PUBLIC-PRIVATE PARTNERSHIP FOR HOMELAND SECURITY

The private sector is and should be an integral part of any effort to advance homeland security. But in the end, protecting the nation and its citizens is a core responsibility of government. Identifying just where the responsibilities for the private versus public sectors start and stop and where they overlap is largely uncharted territory. For most of the post–World War II era, defending the nation against those who might threaten it was accomplished by forging alliances and deploying U.S. armed forces beyond U.S. shores. Everyday citizens and companies were essentially free to go about their lives focused on maximizing their personal and commercial interests. The new threat environment highlighted by the 9/11 attacks has changed that.

A necessary stepping-off point for defining the appropriate security role for the private sector is to clarify what the market can and cannot do on its own when it comes to homeland security. Below are some guiding principles that should inform Washington's efforts.

THE GOVERNMENT AS A MARKET PLAYER

The government itself is a major market player whose actions condition what the private sector can and will do when it comes to security. Policymakers, legislators, and senior federal managers must actively work toward eliminating disincentives and providing incentives that encourage private entities to embrace the homeland security imperative.
As mentioned previously in this report, the White House's 2002 *National Strategy for Homeland Security* has assigned lead responsibility for protecting the nation's critical infrastructures to the market: "The government should only address those activities that the market does not adequately provide—for example, national defense or border security….For other aspects of homeland security, sufficient incentives exist in the private market to supply protection." However, the government is unavoidably a

prominent market player before, during, and after a major security incident. Its everyday activities—regulation, oversight, enforcement, spending, and investments—condition, constrain, or enable what the private sector can and will do.

For instance, the free market choice of a major financial firm wanting to build an emergency operations center as a backup for its headquarters might be to locate it in an overseas office where much of the infrastructure and skilled staff are already in place. But bank regulators might not permit that because they lack the jurisdiction to oversee those operations outside the United States. Or a company might want to devise a contingency plan where it deploys its experts from around the globe in response to an incident to help quickly restore a critical system. But this plan will not work if a company's experts cannot clear immigration because of tightened border security or if they cannot get past local law enforcement security control points established around the perimeter of a disaster zone.

In the aftermath of a disaster, CEOs know that the security environment they might aspire to create today will be transformed. Following a disaster, Washington has a near-perfect track record, regardless of which political party has been in charge, of rushing to enact new laws and regulations to address perceived deficiencies. The government's latent power to change the rules, particularly when security is involved, works as a chill on private sector investment in long-term strategic solutions. It is hard to justify costly expenditures to put in place new capabilities when there is a significant risk that requirements may change overnight after a terrorist strike. Alternatively, the compassionate federal impulse to provide emergency assistance to the victims of disasters affects the market's approach to managing its exposure to risk. Some company executives may decide to live with suboptimal security if they believe that, in the end, the government will help them out should the worst come to pass.

Perhaps most importantly, the government has a unique ability to provide several things that cannot be provided by the private market. First, intelligence and law enforcement agencies have most of the information on terrorist threats that could allow the market better to align its investments with risk. Second, only the government has the authority to enforce compliance with agreed-upon standards. Without a credible risk of enforcement, company executives may be reluctant to incur the costs associated with new security measures out of a concern that they could be placed at a competitive disadvantage relative to other companies that do not pursue such measures. Finally, companies that make a good-faith effort to undertake antiterrorist measures face liability risk should terrorists succeed at defeating those measures. Only government can create the legal mechanisms to place limits on liability exposure.

In short, before, during, and after a terrorist attack, the federal government must be a fully engaged partner that is constantly aware of how its activities can affect how companies approach security.

THE PRIVATE SECTOR AS A RESOURCE

The private sector is not just a target, but a resource.

The private sector is in a position to provide information, capabilities, and assets that the government does not possess, which would help improve homeland security. For example, in Hong Kong, privately owned marine terminal operators have invested their own resources into developing ways that radiation detection portals and container imaging equipment can be integrated into the design of their entry gates so as to support inspections without slowing their operations. As a result, they have demonstrated that it is possible to screen every container for a weapon of mass destruction versus the current government approach of relying on limited intelligence to examine only a select few. In the aftermath of a disaster, the private sector has demonstrated how it can play an important role providing essential materials, assets, and logistics, as it did in response to the Asian tsunami and Hurricane Katrina. Additionally, the private sector is essential to providing surge capacity in critical supplies like health care (vaccines, generators, hospital beds, etc.) or highly specialized and hard-to-replace equipment, like electric transformers, which are needed to provide basic electric service. The government must fully integrate private sector assets into its response and recovery plans and be willing to be the purchaser of last resort for critical supplies that might otherwise not be readily available during an emergency. To this end, the government must support the stockpiling of certain assets and also support the ability of the private sector to produce critical assets rapidly that may be needed but that have not been stockpiled.

PRIVATE SECTOR DIVERSITY

The private sector is not monolithic. Federal homeland security efforts need to better address the private sector's dynamism and complexity.

Too often public officials speak about the private sector as if it were a single actor. One of the hallmarks of America's private sector is its diversity, ranging from the Fortune 500 to hundreds of thousands of small- and medium-sized businesses. The government's ability to work in partnership with industry on security matters is directly related to its ability to understand how the private sector works.

The consequences of terrorist attacks on critical infrastructure vary widely by sector. Chemical, nuclear, oil, and gas facilities may make an attractive target for terrorists because these facilities themselves can be turned into weapons of mass destruction. A successful attack could result in hundreds of thousands of casualties. Transportation conveyances carrying hazardous cargoes potentially can be used both as weapons and as a weapons-delivery system, generating death and destruction while simultaneously generating cascading economic consequences. For instance, should a cargo container deliver a smuggled radiation dispersal device ("dirty bomb") into the heart of a U.S. city and be detonated, other cities would become alarmed that the trucks, trains, and ships within their jurisdiction may pose a similar risk. The process of stopping and examining the hundreds of thousands of containers located within the United States on any given day would quickly generate gridlock throughout the global intermodal transportation system, effectively severing the logistical lifelines for manufactures and retailers worldwide. In a similar fashion, should the food supply system be used to deliver poisons or disease, the entire sector would be affected while authorities sought to identify where the breach of security occurred. Then there are infrastructures, such as the electric power grid and information systems, that if targeted would probably not lead to substantial immediate loss of life. Their appeal as targets stems from the potential to inflict substantial harm and social disruption, since they are critical to the health of multiple sectors. The nature of the danger associated with targeting each sector should inform the security measures taken to prevent or mitigate the consequences of a successful attack.

Some critical infrastructure sectors are more prepared than others.

Every sector did not begin at the same security starting point on 9/11. The nuclear power industry always has been viewed as a potential target and is closely regulated so that substantial physical security measures and contingency plans are in place. Finance and IT systems are under daily attack by sophisticated hackers and criminals. As a result, protective measures and protocols for managing cyberattacks are fairly well established and can be sustained without regulation. But the chemical industry has historically worried about accidents and not about intentional attacks. Chemical facilities are often located near major population centers and adjacent to other important infrastructures, but they were never designed to be hardened and secure. Another very vulnerable sector is the food industry. A bioterrorism attack on food distribution or processing centers would likely result in a chaotic national response because so many agencies and jurisdictions would be involved and so little work has been done to coordinate in advance their postincident roles. Recognizing and adapting to the varying levels of security maturity and immaturity among critical sectors is a necessary starting point for homeland security officials.

An appreciation for where the greatest amount of work needs to be done should inform the setting of the federal government's priorities. More specifically, the government should focus its efforts on those industries in which there is the greatest gap between consequences and the current state of preparedness to prevent and recover quickly from attack should prevention measures fail.

The private sector will invest in security on its own, but when voluntary action is insufficient, government involvement is necessary and desirable.

The private sector is clearly willing to make investments—up to a point—that can make the nation more secure. Finance and IT companies willingly secure themselves against cyberthreats. Large chemical companies have invested nearly $3 billion since 9/11 to upgrade security. Marine terminal operators and ocean carriers have been participating actively in container security pilot programs. In some instances, these efforts may be sufficient to address terrorist threats. But government policies must acknowledge the variations in market incentives, business models, and investment cycles among the sectors in determining how much security industries can and will provide on their own. While nonregulatory approaches are often preferable, lawmakers and regulators may need to weigh in when it is clear that industry, despite even good-faith efforts, cannot get the job done. Specifically, the federal government may need to step in to ensure uniformity and enforcement of standards to provide a predictable regime that allows companies to make security investments without fear that such efforts will prove obsolete or insufficient if the government imposes future requirements. Government regulation is not always in conflict with the best interests of the private sector. In many cases it can help to bound market uncertainties, making it easier for markets to work and for the private sector to make investment decisions.

How Much Security is Enough?

Company executives are apprehensive about their own ability to decide how much security is enough. Should their companies be targeted or exploited by terrorists, some worry they will not be given credit for safeguards they put in place but instead will be blamed for not having done enough.

Arriving at the optimal balance between investment and return requires first identifying the threat that the security measure is designed to counter. To the extent that there is detailed threat information, it is typically known only to the government. Therefore, the public sector must be willing to share that threat information with private companies if it expects them to make an appropriate decision about the security investments they should be undertaking. The federal government also needs to recognize good-faith efforts publicly when companies make them and provide some level of "Good Samaritan" protections if those efforts fall short. Purely voluntary protective efforts can expose a company to the claim that it was aware of its vulnerabilities but cut corners in addressing them. Without liability safeguards, executives will face pressure to limit company efforts to acknowledge and address security concerns.

INTERNATIONAL SECURITY STANDARDS

Security efforts in a number of critical infrastructure sectors are deeply affected by international competition and the existence or lack of international standards. The federal government has a unique ability through diplomacy to speed the development of international standards that can benefit security efforts by U.S. companies.

Private sector efforts to improve security at their facilities are frequently constrained not only by cost concerns and free-rider issues relative to U.S. competitors, but also relative to international competitors. For example, there is no requirement at ports for employee identification cards, and progress on credentialing has been hindered by, in part, lack of progress in international negotiations to create a global standard. Additionally, there is no comprehensive system to check containers as they are loaded overseas and to seal them to ensure that they have not been tampered with. New domestically imposed security measures that are not adopted by industry counterparts overseas can raise the costs and undermine the competitiveness of U.S. companies. Meanwhile, the gaps in security abroad may still threaten the operations of enterprises within the United States. For instance, an attack on a compressor station at the start of a natural gas pipeline in Canada may lead to power outages in the United States as power plants are starved of the imported natural gas. Efforts to harmonize standards and requirements internationally benefit from sustained government action on all fronts, including public, bilateral, and multilateral diplomacy. While companies can help to identify optimal solutions, negotiating global standards requires the active participation of federal officials from the U.S. Department of State and a number of other federal departments.

GOOD CORPORATE CITIZENSHIP

Private sector executives are not driven purely by economics, but also by patriotism and civic duty. The federal government needs to do a better job in finding ways to channel companies' civic-mindedness.

Innovative initiatives like the New Jersey Business Force Program and the Eden Prairie (Minnesota) Safe and Secure City Program demonstrate that business leaders are not just narrowly focused on bottom-line profits.[20] These programs provide an organizational framework for state and local governments to partner with leading companies to heighten awareness and to prepare for terrorist and other high-consequence events. U.S. companies are willing to commit substantial time, expertise, and resources to support the homeland security mission as an act of enlightened self-interest and community service. The federal government must make a concerted effort to recognize and encourage this behavior and support the imitation and rapid adoption of successful partnering initiatives by other communities.

ROLE OF THE INSURANCE MARKET

The insurance market can help inform and encourage private enterprises to invest in measures that make them resilient and secure. However, for that potential to be realized fully, the government must play an active role.

Given the distinctive qualities of terrorism risk, the private sector alone cannot provide a market for insuring against terrorist acts. U.S. intelligence as opposed to exclusive reliance on actuarial data and predictive models needs to inform estimates about the

---

[20] Authors' interview with Michael Laden, president of Trade Innovations Inc., September 20, 2005.

nature and frequency of the threat. Since large-scale events could lead to ruinous losses and insolvency, even major insurance companies are understandably hesitant to provide coverage without some participation of the government in the terrorism insurance market. The federal government's participation in the market must involve sharing threat information, certifying when a particular event qualifies as a terrorist act, supporting the development of security best practices and standards, and providing a last-resort financial backstop for claims that exceed an agreed-upon threshold.

RECOMMENDATIONS

The federal government needs urgently to undertake steps to ensure that critical infrastructures are better protected and that preparedness, response, and recovery efforts are ready to leverage fully all available assets, including those owned by the private sector. In order to do so, Washington must use a full range of policy tools to engender true public-private partnership for homeland security. The federal government must exert greater leadership; establish national priorities; strengthen DHS; provide better threat information; aid the development of security best practices and standards; provide incentives for greater private sector security investment; establish liability protections; integrate private assets and capabilities into preparedness, response and recovery; support the creation of stockpiles or surge capacity for certain critical supplies; and recognize security efforts and innovation that have occurred in the private sector. The following ten steps detail these recommendations and their potential benefits.

FEDERAL POLICY PARADIGM

Change the federal policy paradigm. The federal government must be an equal partner in securing critical infrastructures and must provide leadership, not followership.

Washington needs to recognize that the current policy paradigm for critical infrastructure protection is flawed because it assumes that the market will provide adequate incentives for security investments and assigns only a limited support role to the federal government. Security is a public good, and as such, the market will not provide sufficient incentives. The private sector wants and needs the public sector to provide active leadership and coordinated and sustained engagement in crafting policies, identifying and enforcing common security standards, and providing economic incentives for embracing those standards.

Complete the national prioritization of critical infrastructure, but do not let completion delay immediate efforts to improve security where known security gaps exist.

Because it is unlikely that DHS will be able to complete the prioritization of critical infrastructure and develop a national protective plan by the end of 2006, Congress should commission a rapid-turnaround study to be performed by the National Academy of Sciences supported with the assistance of a top-tier private sector management consulting firm. Such a study would prioritize sectors by risk and also seek to rank protective measures recommended in earlier work by the National Academies based on cost-benefit and other analytical methods. These evaluations should be conducted both within each major sector and across the sectors so as to identify important interdependencies. Once this prioritization has been completed, it should be used to guide the federal allocation of resources, to keep track of federal and private sector protective efforts, and to determine how such efforts have improved U.S. homeland security posture.

While prioritization of critical infrastructure is essential as a tool for long-term planning and accountability, completion of that effort should not be allowed to delay undertaking protective measures now in sectors that are known to pose significant risks.

STRENGTHENING DEPARTMENT OF HOMELAND SECURITY PERSONNEL

Strengthen the quality and experience of DHS and establish a personnel exchange program with the private sector to help make DHS a more effective partner to the private sector.

DHS has been struggling to fulfill its homeland security mission in no small part because of difficulties in creating a stable, experienced, and technically knowledgeable professional cadre of managers. DHS is relying on personnel from its component agencies, detailees from other agencies, and private contractors to provide most of the civil service backbone to fill the new positions created at its headquarters. DHS's legacy agencies have been raided to fill DHS management ranks, and too much of DHS's essential policy and strategy work is being outsourced to contractors. For personnel seconded from other federal agencies, their primary organizational loyalty remains with the parent agency to which they are likely to return. That has led to the worryingly high turnover of DHS management personnel. Making matters worse, DHS is struggling to attract the most qualified personnel because it is not viewed as a rewarding place to work. Personnel issues disrupt DHS's capacity to manage long-term initiatives. If this situation continues, DHS will remain an unacceptably weak federal department for a decade or more.

Congress should provide for appropriate billets for permanent senior civil service government employees modeled on the office of the secretary of defense. It should provide the secretary of homeland security with maximum ability to attract and retain seasoned personnel, and DHS should actively recruit candidates with private sector experience or deep knowledge of industry. As part of that effort, DHS should establish a personnel exchange program between the private sector and DHS. Such a program would allow industry experts and managers to take a leave of absence from their companies to serve in government while DHS employees with expertise in infrastructure protection, information sharing, and response and recovery could spend time out of government working in the operations of a private enterprise. A prestigious, high-visibility public-private exchange program of this nature could help build mutual understanding and greater trust between the federal homeland security agencies and the private sector. The program could be modeled on programs at the Federal Reserve banks where private sector personnel, with the support of their employers, apply for highly competitive opportunities to serve in the Fed for one to two years.

INFORMATION SHARING

Move beyond talking about the need to dramatically improve information sharing with the private sector and hold government officials accountable for actually doing it.

The government must follow through on numerous recommendations that have been made since 9/11 to improve information sharing with the private sector.[21] To build productive information-sharing relationships, government and the private sector should establish standing and formal trusted-information sharing and analysis processes. Government should explore ways to better integrate industry into the full government intelligence cycle—requirements, tasking, analysis, reporting, and dissemination—both as a consumer and a potential provider of information. The government should increase the ability of the private sector to receive data directly from the most reliable threat and vulnerability sources. There should be a comprehensive and coordinated national plan to facilitate critical infrastructure-protection information sharing that clearly delineates roles and responsibilities, defines interim objectives and milestones, sets time frames for achieving objectives, and establishes performance measures. The White House and Congress need to hold the relevant agency heads accountable for carrying out this vital agenda.

STANDARDS AND REGULATIONS

Work with industry to establish security standards and implement regulations where necessary and where industry seeks them.

The federal government should develop security best practices and standards in concert with industry, especially where industries are advocating greater government involvement (chemicals, maritime transportation) and in industries where interdependencies in fragmented markets (electrical power generation, surface transport,

---

[21] For examples of recommendations, see Harold C. Ralyea and Jeffrey W. Seifert, *Information Sharing for Homeland Security: A Brief Overview*, RL32597, Congressional Research Service, updated September 30, 2004, pp. 22–25, available at http://www.fas.org/sgp/crs/RL32597.pdf; U.S. General Accounting Office, *Critical Infrastructure Protection: Establishing Effective Information Sharing with Infrastructure Sectors, Testimony*, GAO-04-699T, April 21, 2004, available at http://www.gao.gov/new.items/d04699t.pdf; U.S. General Accounting Office, *Critical Infrastructure Protection: Improving Information Sharing with Infrastructure Sectors, Report to Congressional Requesters*, GAO-04-780, July 2004, available at http://www.gao.gov/new.items/d04780.pdf; ISAC Council, "A Functional Model for Critical Infrastructure Information Sharing and Analysis: Maturing and Expanding Efforts," White Paper, January 31, 2004, available at http://www.isaccouncil.org/pub/Information_Sharing_and_Analysis_013104.pdf; and ISAC Council, "Government–Private Sector Relations," White Paper, January 31, 2004, available at http://www.isaccouncil.org/pub/Government_Private_Sector_Relations_013104.pdf.

and food sectors) make it appropriate. To the extent that the government develops and seeks to enforce best practices and standards, such practices should be tested within commercial environments before they are applied broadly. Several measures will be essential to the success of such a program. First, Congress must redress the general lack of regulatory authority granted to the Department of Homeland Security. While the Homeland Security Act gave DHS broad security responsibilities, it largely failed to grant DHS authority to regulate and enforce security.[22] Second, DHS efforts to work with industry to develop standards will be greatly improved by strengthening the private sector experience and industry-specific knowledge of DHS employees. That can be achieved by pursuing the personnel, recruitment, and human capital exchange programs discussed in the third recommendation. Finally, it is always more effective to embed adequate security protocols in critical infrastructure during the design and construction phases. Therefore, the federal government should promote more secure and resilient infrastructure nationally by making federal funding for new infrastructure or upgrades to existing infrastructure contingent on the adoption of security standards.

TAX INCENTIVES

Use targeted tax incentives to promote investments in security and resiliency in the highest-risk industries.

The federal government should use tax incentives to promote private sector investments in security and resiliency that would not otherwise be undertaken. For example, tax credits could be made available to companies that make investments to improve chemical security, since voluntary investments by chemical manufacturers are acknowledged to be insufficient. Tax credits could also be made available to support company efforts to build redundancy into supply-chain and other delivery systems that are critical to the functioning of the U.S. economy, including electric power transmission and the delivery of oil and gas and food and water. Historically, supply-chain and other delivery systems

---

[22] U.S. Congress, *Homeland Security Act of 2002*, 107th Congress, 2nd Session, 2002, see section 877 regarding limitations on the Department of Homeland Security's regulatory authority. Available at http://files.findlaw.com/news.findlaw.com/hdocs/docs/terrorism/hsa2002.pdf.

have been designed to be low cost and efficient. Federal tax policies could enable companies to invest greater amounts in the redundancy and recoverability of such systems, making the American economy and society more resilient in the face of terrorist attacks.

Additionally, tax credits could be provided that promote the adoption of terrorism insurance by companies. Tax credits for insurance premiums could help increase insurance coverage in sectors such as chemicals, energy, and transport, which pose among the highest critical infrastructure risks, but have the lowest rates of terrorism-insurance adoption.[23]

Eligibility for security-related tax breaks obviously should be aligned with federal critical infrastructure priorities and an assessment of each proposal's viability. Additionally, tax credits could be made available only for a limited number of years and on a declining-scale basis to speed the adoption of security efforts in the near term.

FEDERAL LIABILITY PROTECTIONS

Make companies that undertake security improvements eligible for federal liability protections.

A lack of liability protections acts as a disincentive for companies to pursue security measures. That is because purely voluntary protective efforts can expose companies to claims that they were aware of their vulnerabilities but were negligent in taking *sufficient* measures to address them. In the aftermath of a terrorist attack, owners and operators of critical infrastructure should be shielded from lawsuits if they made good-faith efforts to abide by agreed-upon security protocols, even if these efforts still prove insufficient to prevent an attack by determined terrorists. Similar to the Safety Act, which limits liability for manufacturers of homeland security products, Congress should provide appropriate liability protections for companies that meet or exceed baseline security measures established by the federal government for eligible critical infrastructure sectors. At the

---

[23] Marsh and McLennan Companies, "Marketwatch: Terrorism Insurance 2005; Industry Focus: Chemicals," 2005, see http://solutions.marsh.com/TRIA/documents/Marshs_Marketwatch_Terrorism_-_Chemicals_Industry.pdf.

same time, the federal government should improve its implementation of the Safety Act by shortening the time it takes for companies to qualify homeland security technologies for liability protection.[24]

PRACTICE MAKES PERFECT

Substantially increase the number of tabletop and field exercises for responding to catastrophic events and integrate private sector companies both into those exercises and into regionally based emergency planning.

One of the most helpful ways to identify gaps within existing plans, develop improved protocols, and generate political and private sector buy-in to address shortcomings is to conduct comprehensive training exercises. The private sector possesses extraordinary logistics capabilities to swiftly direct transportation assets, people, and goods where they are most needed. Through their around-the-clock operations centers, senior managers in many large corporations often have the ability to collect critical information at or near the scene of major incidents when local sources of official information may not be available. Homeland security planners should not wait until disaster strikes before efforts are made to tap the latent capabilities the private sector can bring to the table.

The Department of Homeland Security should work with the U.S. Department of Defense to design annual exercises, to be held in every region of the country. An emphasis should be placed on high-consequence events that affect multiple critical sectors concurrently. The congressionally mandated Top Officials (TOPOFF) exercise should be stepped up from a biannual event to an annual exercise and be used to ensure that the nation has the ability to simultaneously manage two concurrent major catastrophic events, including terrorist attacks and natural disasters. The exercises should fully integrate the participation of the private sector, identifying private sector targets, assets, and capabilities ahead of time and integrating them into these exercises. That

---

[24] Tim Starks, "Best Laid Plans: Effort to Lure Homeland Businesses with Liability Protection Falls Far Short of Goals," *Congressional Quarterly*, January 7, 2005.

should lead, over time, to the deeper integration of the private sector into national and regional response and recovery plans.

SUPPLIES AND CAPABILITIES FOR RESPONDING TO TERRORIST ATTACKS

Identify specialized supplies/capabilities that will be in short supply following certain types of terrorist incidents and other high-consequence events. Develop plans with the private sector to ensure the availability of these specialized supplies/capabilities.

The federal government should identify certain specialized supplies and capabilities— vaccines, ventilators, hospital surge capacity, laboratory capacity, decontamination equipment, electric transformers—that are likely to be critical but in short supply in the aftermath of various terrorist attacks or other high-consequence events such as a pandemic flu outbreak or natural disaster. The government should actively work with the private sector to stockpile these supplies, or it should work to enhance the private sector's capacity to rapidly provide them when there is no viable commercial market.[25] To better prepare for mass-casualty events and other major medical emergencies, the National Academies' Institute of Medicine should be funded to convene an expert working group charged with identifying these supplies and capabilities and estimating the cost to the government of purchasing them or building the spare capacity to supply them on a rapid basis. In addition, the government should build on lessons learned from various pilot public-private partnerships to integrate private sector assets, know-how, and personnel into ensuring that scarce critical supplies/capabilities are available when needed.

---

[25] House Select Committee on Homeland Security, *Beyond Anthrax: Confronting the Future Biological Weapons Threat*, May 2004, see http://knxas1.hsdl.org/homesec/docs/legis/nps03-051304-14.pdf; Joe McDade, "Biodefense Wake-up Call," *Washington Times*, October 18, 2004, see http://www.washtimes.com/op-ed/20041017-102446-8696r.htm. Both pieces advocate significant federal investments in the private sector's capacity to develop responses more rapidly to unforeseen viruses.

Establish a federal awards program that recognizes private sector efforts and innovation in homeland security.

A federal award program should be established that recognizes the innovation, efforts, and contributions of the private sector toward improving homeland security. A model is the prestigious Baldridge National Quality Awards program, a public-private partnership established to recognize excellence in corporate practices. The awards should particularly focus on critical infrastructure protection, information sharing, and response and recovery. The award criteria should be weighted toward industry efforts to improve the security of their own assets; to increase security collaboration within and across sectors; and to increase homeland security collaboration with federal, state, and local government and nongovernmental organizations (NGOs). An awards program would appropriately provide public recognition for the patriotism, goodwill, and creativity of companies. The publicity associated with the program would also provide a means to highlight valuable and innovative efforts that might otherwise go unnoticed, thereby encouraging their adoption by other companies and sectors. Companies would likely respond well to the opportunity to publicize and market their security achievements.

CONCLUSION

The task we set for the working group meetings and in drafting this report was to identify problems and to provide reasonable recommendations for addressing them. The remedies we offer require only a White House and a Congress committed to making meaningful changes. But in most cases, these recommendations are still first steps. They will not by themselves close the gap between where we are and where we need to be in order to secure the nation. The risk of catastrophic terrorist attacks and cascading security, economic, and social consequences will remain as long as Washington fails to mobilize the private sector and civil society in a national effort to make the United States more secure, more prepared, and more resilient.

The Defense Department, in its recent Quadrennial Defense Review, began with a simple statement: "The United States is a nation engaged in what will be a long war." In the fifth year of this long war, the nation's state of preparedness should be much higher. It is long past the time when we truly engage our private industry and private citizens in this struggle. In his first budget message after 9/11, President George W. Bush reminded the nation that not since World War II have our values and our way of life been so threatened. But in that war that ended half a century ago, it was not just the military that was called upon to fight. Gray-haired executives traded in pinstripe suits for uniforms to organize our defenses at home; factories stopped making cars and started making weapons and munitions; and mothers left their children in the care of neighbors and relatives so that they could work the assembly lines. As a nation, we were forever changed by the experience. Recognizing this parallel, the president has called homeland security "our new national calling." Sadly, national efforts to date on homeland security are nowhere near the kind of effort this nation can produce when called to service.

The enemies we face are no match for American spirit, ingenuity, and courage. But only when we marshal these qualities in our current struggle with radical jihadi will our adversaries become impotent. The private sector can and must play an indispensable role in addressing the many problems that have plagued the nation's homeland security efforts. But the federal government must be willing and able to enlist that help and provide leadership for those efforts.

APPENDIX

APPENDIX

PRIVATE SECTOR ADVISORY COMMITTEE

EMILY ALTMAN
Managing Director and Head of
    International Government
JPMorgan Chase & Co.

PHIL ANDERSON
Vice President, Washington Operations
Lucent Technologies

JEFFREY BEWKES
President and COO
Time Warner Inc.

RICHARD T. BISTRONG
Vice President, International Sales &
    Marketing
Armor Holdings, Inc.

KAY BOULWARE-MILLER
Managing Counsel
Merck & Co., Inc.

PAUL D. BURGESS
Executive Speechwriter
Northrop Grumman Corporation

MIC CHANDRANI
Senior Vice President, Global Security
American Express Company

EDWARD T. CLOONAN
Vice President, International &
    Corporate Affairs
American International Group, Inc.

LUC DE CLAPIERS
President and CEO
IXIS Capital Markets

ROBERT C. DINERSTEIN
Vice Chairman, Americas
UBS Investment Bank

DANIEL S. DREYFUS
Senior Associate
Booz Allen Hamilton Inc.

JACQUES DUBOIS
Chairman and CEO
Swiss Re America Holding Corporation

JAMES A. EUCHNER
Vice President, Advanced Concepts &
    Technology and Chief e-Business
    Officer
Pitney Bowes Inc.

ELLIOT J. FELDMAN
Partner; National Leader, Global Practices;
    and National Leader, International
    Trade, Customs, & Immigration
Baker & Hostetler LLP

MARK FISCH
Managing Partner
Continental Properties

DAVID FUHRMANN
Partner
Glenwood LLC

MARTIN J. GROSS
President
Sandalwood Securities, Inc.

PATRICK E. KELLEHER
Managing Director, Worldwide Security
Merrill Lynch & Co., Inc.

CHRISTOPHER M. KELLY
Vice President
Booz Allen Hamilton Inc.

WILLIAM P. KINANE
Vice President, International Division
Guardsmark LLC

HENRY R. KRAVIS
Founding Partner
Kohlberg Kravis Roberts & Co.

IRA A. LIPMAN
Founder and Chairman
Guardsmark LLC

SUSAN MARAGHY
Vice President for Homeland Security,
    IT & Civil Agencies
Lockheed Martin Corporation

ROBERT L. MCCLURE
Regional Director
Business Executives for National Security

GARY MILLER
Manager
The Boeing Company

RICHARD S. MILLER
President, Government Solutions
Lucent Technologies

DAVID T. NASSEF
Vice President, Federal Relations
Pitney Bowes Inc.

RICHARD L. PLEPLER
Executive Vice President
Home Box Office

RON PROSSOR
Vice President, Defense Systems
The Boeing Company

ALFRED J. PUCHALA JR.
Managing Director
Signal Equity Partners

ALAN RIDGE
Director of International Sales
Armor Holdings, Inc.

JEFFREY A. ROSEN
Deputy Chairman
Lazard

BERNARD L. SCHWARTZ
Chairman and CEO
BLS Investments, LLC

STEPHEN J. SCOTT
President
Scott International, Inc.

JOHN C. STAMMREICH
Vice President, Homeland Security-
    Phantom Security
The Boeing Company

GORDON C. STEWART
President
Insurance Information Institute

ENZO VISCUSI
Group Senior Vice President
Eni S.p.A.

MARK WELLING
Managing Partner
Allen & Overy LLP

HERBERT S. WINOKUR JR.
Chairman and CEO
Capricorn Holdings, LLC

ABOUT THE AUTHORS

Stephen E. Flynn is the author of the critically acclaimed national best seller, *America the Vulnerable*. He is the inaugural occupant of the Jeane J. Kirkpatrick chair in national security studies at the Council on Foreign Relations. Dr. Flynn served as director and principal author for the Task Force report *"America: Still Unprepared—Still in Danger,"* chaired by former Senators Gary Hart and Warren Rudman. Since 9/11, he has provided congressional testimony on homeland security matters on seventeen occasions. He spent twenty years as a commissioned officer in the U.S. Coast Guard, including two commands at sea; served in the White House Military Office during the George H. W. Bush administration; and was director for global issues on the National Security Council staff during the Clinton administration. He holds a PhD and MALD from the Fletcher School of Law and Diplomacy and a BS from the U.S. Coast Guard Academy.

Daniel B. Prieto is director of the Homeland Security Center at the Reform Institute. Previously, he was research director of the Homeland Security Partnership Initiative and fellow at the Belfer Center for Science and International Affairs at Harvard University's John F. Kennedy School of Government. He has served on the professional staff of the Select Committee on Homeland Security in the U.S. House of Representatives and is a former technology-industry executive and investment banker. Mr. Prieto is a recipient of the International Affairs Fellowship from the Council on Foreign Relations, a member of the Council on Foreign Relations, and an associate member of the Markle Foundation Task Force on national security in the information age. He holds an MA from the Johns Hopkins University School of Advanced International Studies (SAIS) and a BA from Wesleyan University.

OTHER COUNCIL SPECIAL REPORTS
SPONSORED BY THE COUNCIL ON FOREIGN RELATIONS

Afghanistan's Uncertain Transition from Turmoil to Normalcy
Barnett R. Rubin; CSR No. 12, March 2006

Preventing Catastrophic Nuclear Terrorism
Charles D. Ferguson; CSR No.11, March 2006

Getting Serious About the Twin Deficits
Menzie D. Chinn; CSR No. 10, September 2005

Both Sides of the Aisle: A Call for Bipartisan Foreign Policy
Nancy E. Roman; CSR No. 9, September 2005

Forgotten Intervention? What the United States Needs to Do in the Western Balkans
Amelia Branczik and William L. Nash; CSR No. 8, June 2005

A New Beginning: Strategies for a More Fruitful Dialogue with the Muslim World
Craig Charney and Nicole Yakatan; CSR No. 7, May 2005

Power-Sharing in Iraq
David L. Phillips; CSR No. 6, April 2005

Giving Meaning to "Never Again": Seeking an Effective Response to the Crisis in Darfur and Beyond
Cheryl O. Igiri and Princeton N. Lyman; CSR No. 5, September 2004

Freedom, Prosperity, and Security: The G8 Partnership with Africa: Sea Island 2004 and Beyond
J. Brian Atwood, Robert S. Browne, and Princeton N. Lyman; CSR No. 4, May 2004

Addressing the HIV/AIDS Pandemic: A U.S. Global AIDS Strategy for the Long Term
Daniel M. Fox and Princeton N. Lyman; CSR No. 3, May 2004
Cosponsored with the Milbank Memorial Fund

Challenges for a Post-Election Philippines
Catharin E. Dalpino; CSR No. 2, May 2004

Stability, Security, and Sovereignty in the Republic of Georgia
David L. Phillips; CSR No. 1, January 2004

To order a hard copy, please call the Brookings Institution Press: 800-537-5487.
Note: Council Special Reports are available on the Council's website at www.cfr.org, along with a complete list of the Council publications since 1998. For more information, contact publications@cfr.org.